BALANCING YOGA

BY LAURA VILLANO, RYT
ILLUSTRATED BY CHRISTOS SKALTSAS

BLUE OWL
BOOKS

TIPS FOR CAREGIVERS

The practice of yoga helps us learn about our breath and body, how the two are connected, and how they can help us acknowledge our feelings without letting them overwhelm us. This awareness can help us navigate different situations at school or at home. Yoga gives us tools to be the best versions of ourselves in every situation. Plus, moving our bodies feels good!

SOCIAL AND EMOTIONAL GOALS

After reading this book, kids will be able to use their yoga practice to:

1. Become more aware of their emotions and the physical sensations they produce in the body (self-awareness).

2. Use the techniques included in the text to help manage their emotions and de-stress (self-management).

TIPS FOR PRACTICE

Encourage self-awareness and self-management with these prompts:

Before reading: Ask students to check in with themselves. How do they feel, in both mind and body?
Emotional example: What kinds of thoughts are you having?
Physical example: How does your body feel today?

During reading: Encourage students to check in as they move through the book.
Emotional example: How does it feel when you close your eyes and focus on your breathing?
Physical example: How do certain poses feel in your body?

After reading: Take time to reflect after practicing the poses.
Emotional example: How do you feel after practicing yoga?
Physical example: Are there certain poses you like or don't like?

TABLE OF CONTENTS

BEFORE YOU BEGIN YOUR PRACTICE, YOU WILL NEED:

- Yoga mat (A towel or blanket works, too!)
- Comfy clothes so you can move around easily
- Wall or chair close by
- Water to stay hydrated
- A good attitude and an open mind!

By practicing the poses in this book, you understand any physical activity has some risk of injury.
If you experience pain or discomfort, please listen to your body, discontinue activity, and ask for help.

CHAPTER 1

BREATHING AND BALANCING

Yoga is a **sequence** of body movements. There are many different **poses**. Some we do while seated. Others we do while standing. In this book, you will learn poses that involve balancing!

Before you get started, practice paying attention to your breath. Put your hand on your stomach. **Inhale** through your nose. Feel your belly fill with air. Then **exhale** out of your nose. Feel your belly relax. Repeat this 10 times.

Practice moving your body with your breath.

❯ Reach your arms over your head as you inhale.

❯ Exhale and lower your arms back to your sides.

❯ Repeat this 3 to 5 times.

Focus on moving slowly with your breath into each pose. Let's practice balancing poses!

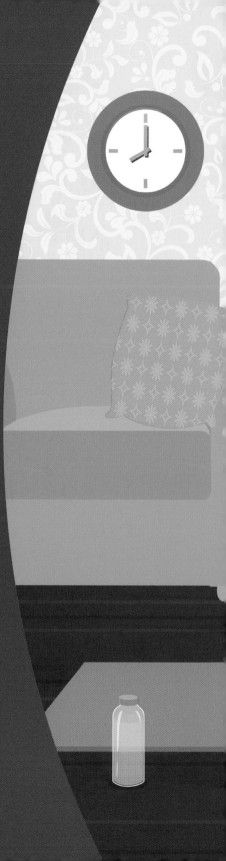

DID YOU KNOW?

Namaste (nah-mah-stay)! This is how we greet each other when we practice yoga. It is a welcoming greeting. When we say it, we place our palms together in front of our chest and slightly bow our head.

CHAPTER 2

PRACTICE THE POSES!

MOUNTAIN POSE

❯ Start on your mat. Stand tall. Plant your feet firmly on the floor.

❯ Keep your arms by your sides. Point your fingertips toward the floor.

❯ Draw your shoulders down your back.

TREE POSE PART 1

❯ Keep your legs **engaged**.

❯ Inhale and lift your left foot.

❯ Rest it flat against your right calf.

TREE POSE PART 2

❯ Slowly touch your palms in front of your heart.

❯ Keep them here for 3 breaths.

❯ Move your foot up to rest against your inner thigh.

❯ Reach your arms overhead. You look like a tree!

❯ Now try the other side. Which leg is easier to balance on?

DID YOU KNOW?

Yoga is a form of exercise. It can help us sleep better and focus. It increases **flexibility** and builds our muscles!

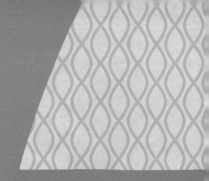

EAGLE POSE

❱ Bend your knees slightly.

❱ Breathe in.

❱ Exhale and wrap your left leg around your right leg.

❱ Cross your right arm over your left.

❱ Bend your elbows and wrap your arms around each other.

❱ Your left fingers should rest on the palm of your right hand.

TIP: Having trouble balancing? Keep your arms reaching out to your sides. Try focusing your eyes on one object.

WARRIOR 3

Let's **flow** from Eagle Pose to Warrior 3!

❯ Inhale, and as you exhale, slowly unwrap your left leg. Reach it straight behind you.

❯ Slowly lean forward.

❯ Unwrap your arms and reach in front of you.

❯ Straighten your balancing leg.

❯ Your body should look like the letter T. Do you feel your right leg muscles working?

❯ Switch. Do Eagle Pose and Warrior 3 on your left side!

TIP: Bend your balancing knee slightly. This keeps all of your muscles working!

FIGURE FOUR POSE

Now let's try Figure Four Pose.

❯ Start by standing tall on your mat.

❯ Slightly bend your knees.

❯ Inhale.

❯ Exhale and cross your left ankle to rest on your right knee.

❯ Your legs should look like the number 4!

❯ Bring your hands together. Touch your palms.

❯ If it feels comfortable, try bending your right knee more or folding forward.

Balancing yoga can be tough. Losing your balance is part of the practice. Have fun with it! Fall out and come back into the pose you are practicing. It is always an option to place a hand on a chair or wall to help balance.

TIP: Take breaks. Your legs are doing a lot of work! Be sure to rest. Focus on your breath between poses.

CHAPTER 3

REFLECT

Slowly make your way to the floor. Lie down on your back. Close your eyes. Inhale and exhale 5 times. Take time to **reflect** on your practice. How do you feel?

How does yoga make you feel for the rest of the day?

GOALS AND TOOLS

GROW WITH GOALS

Practice bringing yoga into your everyday life. This can look different for everyone. Here are some ideas to get you started. You can set your own goals, too! Share your goals with your friends! Friends help us stay on track and meet our goals!

1. Pick the balancing yoga pose that was most challenging. Practice this pose 3 times a week. Take note of how this pose feels the more you do it. What stays the same? What changes?

2. Teach this yoga pose to a family member or friend. Does this provide you with new ways of practicing the pose yourself?

TRY THIS!

Try Warrior 3 with a group!

1. Form a close circle with your classmates or friends.

2. Reach your arms over your neighbors' shoulders. Everyone do this together.

3. Start with your right leg as the balancing leg. As a group, begin to reach your left foot behind you into Warrior 3. Naturally, the group begins to lean forward. Now try the other side!

REFLECT: How did this group Warrior 3 pose compare to Warrior 3 pose on your own? What was challenging about doing yoga as a group? What worked well? What didn't?

GLOSSARY

engaged
Focused on your muscles and keeping them active and strong.

exhale
To breathe out.

flexibility
The ability to bend.

flow
To transition slowly from one yoga pose to another.

focus
To concentrate on something.

inhale
To breathe in.

namaste
A common greeting in yoga. It means, "The spirit in me honors and acknowledges the spirit in you."

poses
Positions or postures.

reflect
To think carefully or seriously about something.

sequence
A series or collection of things that follow each other in a particular order.

yoga
A system of exercises and meditation that helps people control their minds and bodies and become physically fit.

TO LEARN MORE

FACT SURFER

Finding more information is as easy as 1, 2, 3.

1. Go to www.factsurfer.com

2. Enter "**balancingyoga**" into the search box.

3. Choose your cover to see a list of websites.

INDEX

Blue Owl Books are published by Jump!, 5357 Penn Avenue South, Minneapolis, MN 55419, www.jumplibrary.com

Copyright © 2020 Jump! International copyright reserved in all countries. No part of this book may be reproduced in any form without written permission from the publisher.

Library of Congress Cataloging-in-Publication Data

Names: Villano, Laura, author.
Title: Balancing yoga / by Laura Villano.
Description: Blue Owl Books. | Minneapolis, MN: Jump!, Inc., [2020]
Series: Yoga for everyone
Includes index.
Audience: Ages 7–10
Identifiers: LCCN 2019027996 (print)
LCCN 2019027997 (ebook)
ISBN 9781645271819 (hardcover)
ISBN 9781645271826 (paperback)
ISBN 9781645271833 (ebook)
Subjects: LCSH: Hatha yoga for children—Juvenile literature.
Classification: LCC RJ133.7 .V547 2020 (print)
LCC RJ133.7 (ebook)
DDC 613.7/046083—dc23
LC record available at https://lccn.loc.gov/2019027996
LC ebook record available at https://lccn.loc.gov/2019027997

Editor: Jenna Trnka
Designer: Anna Peterson
Illustrator: Christos Skaltsas

Printed in the United States of America at Corporate Graphics in North Mankato, Minnesota.